D1394900

INSPIRATION

FOR

GARDENERS

INSPIRATION FOR GARDENERS

With research by Anna Prudente-Poulton

Summersdale Publishers Ltd
46 West Street
Chichester
West Sussex
PO19 1RP
UK

www.summersdale.com

Printed and bound in the Czech Republic

ISBN: 978-1-84953-634-9

Substantial discounts on bulk quantities of Summersdale books are available to corporations, professional associations and other organisations. For details contact Nicky Douglas by telephone: +44 (0) 1243 756902, fax: +44 (0) 1243 786300 or email: nicky@summersdale.com.

INSPIRATION

FOR

GARDENERS

EMILY DARCY

summersdale

My garden is my most
beautiful masterpiece.

CLAUDE MONET

Even if I knew that tomorrow the world would go to pieces, I would still plant my apple tree.

MARTIN LUTHER

When the world wearies,
and society ceases to satisfy,
there is always the garden.

Minnie Aumonier

Plant the seeds of your dreams now, so that you may harvest them later.

SCOTTIE SOMERS

An addiction to
gardening is not all bad
when you consider all the
other choices in life.

CORA LEA BELL

Those who labour in
the earth are the chosen
people of God.

THOMAS JEFFERSON

I love spring anywhere, but if I could choose I would always greet it in a garden.

RUTH STOUT

Plants want to grow; they are on your side as long as you are reasonably sensible.

ANNE WAREHAM

It didn't occur to me that…
gardening, like music, could
demand practice, patience, a
willingness to make mistakes.

AMY STEWART

One of the healthiest
ways to gamble is with
a spade and a package of
garden seeds.

DAN BENNETT

It was such a pleasure
to sink one's hands into
the warm earth, to feel…
the possibilities of the
new season.

Kate Morton

A weed is a plant that has
mastered every survival skill
except for learning how
to grow in rows.

DOUG LARSON

Do not spread the
compost on the weeds.

WILLIAM SHAKESPEARE

Just to touch the ground is enough for me, even if not a single thing grows from what I plant.

ANDY COUTURIER

Gardening is about
cheating, about persuading
unlikely plants to survive in
unlikely places.

DAVID WHEELER

A garden is a grand teacher. It teaches patience and careful watchfulness; it teaches industry and thrift; above all it teaches entire trust.

GERTRUDE JEKYLL

A good gardener always plants three seeds – one for the bugs, one for the weather and one for himself.

LEO AIKMAN

All gardening is
landscape painting.

WILLIAM KENT

All the wars of the world, all the Caesars, have not the staying power of a lily in a cottage border.

REGINALD FARRER

What is a weed? A plant whose virtues have not yet been discovered.

RALPH WALDO EMERSON

All my life I have tried to pluck a thistle and plant a flower wherever the flower would grow in thought and mind.

ABRAHAM LINCOLN

Bloom where
you're planted!

MARY ENGELBREIT

But each spring… a gardening instinct, sure as the sap rising in the trees, stirs within us.

LEWIS GANNETT

Consider the lilies of the field, how they grow: they neither toil nor spin; and yet I say to you that even Solomon in all his glory was not arrayed like one of these.

MATTHEW 6:28–29

Each flower is a soul
opening out to nature.

GÉRARD DE NERVAL

There is always music amongst the trees in the garden, but our hearts must be very quiet to hear it.

MINNIE AUMONIER

Flowers are beautiful hieroglyphics of nature, with which she indicates how much she loves us.

JOHANN WOLFGANG VON GOETHE

I hold no preference among flowers, so long as they are wild, free, spontaneous.

EDWARD ABBEY

Gardeners, I think,
dream bigger dreams
than emperors.

MARY CANTWELL

I perhaps owe having
become a painter to flowers.

CLAUDE MONET

The garden suggests there
might bc a place where we
can meet nature halfway.

MICHAEL POLLAN

We must cultivate
our garden.

VOLTAIRE

Oh, Adam was a gardener, and God who made him sees That half a proper gardener's work is done upon his knees.

RUDYARD KIPLING

Who loves a garden loves
a greenhouse too.

WILLIAM COWPER

All that in this delightful
Garden grows
Should happy be, and have
immortal bliss.

EDMUND SPENSER

*Si hortum cum bibliotheca
habes, nihil deerit.*

If you have a garden in
your library, you'll have
all you need.

CICERO

April comes like
an idiot, babbling and
strewing flowers.

EDNA ST VINCENT MILLAY

No occupation is so
delightful to me as the
culture of the earth, and no
culture comparable to
that of the garden.

THOMAS JEFFERSON

Weeds are flowers too, once
you get to know them.

A. A. MILNE

In search of my mother's garden, I found my own.

ALICE WALKER

The true meaning of life
is to plant trees, under
whose shade you do not
expect to sit.

NELSON HENDERSON

Gardening is not a
rational act.

MARGARET ATWOOD

Mary always felt that however many years she lived she should never forget that first morning when her garden began to grow.

Frances Hodgson Burnett

Earth is here so kind, that just tickle her with a hoe and she laughs with a harvest.

DOUGLAS WILLIAM JERROLD

A garden never knows
when it's over.

PAULA DEITZ

Compared to gardeners,
I think it is generally agreed
that others understand very
little about anything of
consequence.

HENRY MITCHELL

Finding your garden theme
is as easy as seeing what
brings a smile to your face.

TERESA WATKINS

God Almighty first planted
a garden, the purest of
human pleasures.

FRANCIS BACON

Gardening is always a series
of losses set against a few
triumphs, like life itself.

MAY SARTON

We can complain because rose bushes have thorns, or rejoice because thorn bushes have roses.

ABRAHAM LINCOLN

Half the interest of a garden
is the constant exercise of
the imagination.

MRS C. W. EARLE

I consider every plant hardy
until I have killed it myself.

PETER SMITHERS

What a desolate place
would be a world without
a flower! It would be a face
without a smile, a feast
without a welcome.

Mrs Balfour

If a tree is treated as a living organism, with an understanding of its vital functions, it will be a constant source of profit and pleasure to men.

N. T. MIROV

If you need five tools to
solve a problem in the
garden, four of them will
be easy to find.

MIKE GAROFALO

I have never had so
many good ideas day after
day as when I worked
in the garden.

JOHN ERSKINE

I'm not really a career person. I'm a gardener, basically.

GEORGE HARRISON

In his garden every man may
be his own artist without
apology or explanation.

LOUISE BEEBE WILDER

My garden of flowers is
also my garden of thoughts
and dreams.

ANONYMOUS

In the spring, at the end
of the day, you should
smell like dirt.

MARGARET ATWOOD

Earth laughs in flowers.

RALPH WALDO EMERSON

Grass is the cheapest plant
to install and the most
expensive to maintain.

Pat Howell

It is utterly forbidden
to be half-hearted about
gardening. You have… to
love your garden whether
you like it or not.

W. C. SELLAR
AND R. J. YEATMAN

It's a sign of wisdom that seeds don't squander their energy all at once, instead calmly waiting until the time is right.

MIDAS DEKKERS

I think that if ever a mortal heard the voice of God it would be in a garden at the cool of the day.

Frank Frankfort Moore

We're discovering that
gardening is essential
to human life.

JACQUELINE HÉRITEAU

Where you tend a rose, my lad, a thistle cannot grow.

FRANCES HODGSON BURNETT

'Just living is not enough,'
said the butterfly. 'One must
have sunshine, freedom,
and a little flower.'

HANS CHRISTIAN ANDERSEN

True friendship is like a rose:
we don't realise its beauty
until it fades.

Evelyn Loeb

Of all the wonderful
things… nothing seems to
me more surprising than
the planting of a seed in the
blank earth and the
result thereof.

JULIE MOIR MESSERVY

Where flowers bloom,
so does hope.

LADY BIRD JOHNSON

With a few flowers in my garden, half a dozen pictures and some books, I live without envy.

LOPE DE VEGA

A weed is but an
unloved flower.

ELLA WHEELER WILCOX

One of the most delightful things about a garden is the anticipation it provides.

W. E. JOHNS

Remember that
children, marriage and
flower gardens reflect the
kind of care they get.

H. JACKSON BROWN JR

A garden is a friend you
can visit any time.

ANONYMOUS

The creation of a thousand forests is in one acorn.

RALPH WALDO EMERSON

The great challenge… is not to make the garden look natural, but to make the garden… feel natural.

LAWRENCE HALPRIN

It is only to the gardener that time is a friend, giving each year more than he steals.

BEVERLEY NICHOLS

There are no gardening
mistakes, only experiments.

JANET KILBURN-PHILLIPS

I have great faith in a seed.
Convince me that you
have a seed there, and I am
prepared to expect wonders.

HENRY DAVID THOREAU

The garden is a ground
plot for the mind.

Thomas Hill

Sweet flowers are slow and
weeds make haste.

WILLIAM SHAKESPEARE

There is nothing more agreeable in a garden than good shade, and without it a garden is nothing.

BETTY LANGLEY

Though an old man, I am
but a young gardener.

THOMAS JEFFERSON

To analyse the charms of flowers is like dissecting music; it is one of those things which it is far better to enjoy, than to attempt to fully understand.

HENRY T. TUCKERMAN

Gardens are not made
by sitting in the shade.

RUDYARD KIPLING

All gardeners need to know
when to accept something
wonderful and unexpected.

ALLEN LACY

To plant a garden is to believe in tomorrow.

AUDREY HEPBURN

A garden requires patient
labour and attention… They
thrive because someone
expended effort on them.

LIBERTY HYDE BAILEY

Flowers always make people better, happier and more helpful; they are sunshine, food and medicine to the soul.

LUTHER BURBANK

To dig in one's own earth,
with one's own spade, does
life hold anything better?

BEVERLEY NICHOLS

If you're interested in finding out more about our books, find us on Facebook at **Summersdale Publishers** and follow us on Twitter at **@Summersdale**.

www.summersdale.com